Christmas Recipes Collection

Crock pot, slow cooker, drinks, and cocktail recipes

Hannie P. Scott
www.Hanniepscott.com

Copyright © 2016 Hannie P. Scott
All rights reserved.

No part of this book may be reproduced in any form without written permission from the author. Reviewers may quote brief excerpts from the book in reviews.

Disclaimer: No part of this publication may be reproduced or transmitted in any form, mechanical or electronic, including photocopied or recorded, or by any information storage and retrieval system, or transmitted by email without permission in writing or email from the author or publisher.

While attempts have been made to verify all information provided in this publication, neither the author nor the publisher assumes any responsibility for errors, omissions, or contrary interpretations of the subjects discussed.

This book is for entertainment purposes only. The views expressed are those of the author alone and should not be taken as expert instructions or commands. The reader is responsible for his/her own actions.

Adherence to all applicable laws and regulations, including international, federal, state, and local government, or any other jurisdiction is the sole responsibility of the purchaser or reader.

Neither the author nor the publisher assume any responsibility or liability whatsoever on the behalf of the purchaser or reader of these materials.

ISBN-13: 978-1537683973
ISBN-10: 1537683977

> One of the very nicest things about life is the way we must regularly stop whatever we are doing and devote our attention to eating.

LUCIANO PAVAROTTI

CONTENTS

- Abbreviations 3
- Conversions 3
- BOOK 1: CROCK POT RECIPES 6
- Sausage Breakfast Casserole 7
- French Toast 8
- Cinnamon Pecans 9
- Apple Crisp 10
- Gingerbread Pudding 11
- Carrot Cake 12
- Christmas Crack 13
- Corn Casserole 14
- Sweet Potatoes 15
- Green Beans and New Potatoes 16
- Squash and Apples 17
- Crustless Chicken Pot Pie 18
- Corn Chowder 19
- Turkey Breast 20
- Jambalaya 22
- Easy Christmas Ham 23
- Cranberry Apple Butter 24
- Cornbread Dressing 25
- BOOK 2: SLOW COOKER RECIPES 27
- Pumpkin Spice Oatmeal 28
- Cinnamon Roll Casserole 29
- Candied Pecans 30
- Monkey Bread 31
- Bread Pudding 32
- Fudge 33
- Pumpkin Pie 34

Sweet Potato Mash 35
Cheddar Creamed Corn 36
Sweet Potato Casserole 37
Butternut Squash 38
Hash Brown Casserole 39
Vegetable Stew 40
Baked Potato Soup 41
Chicken and Dumplings 42
Christmas Ham 43
Cranberry Sauce 44
Stuffing 45
Nutella Hot Chocolate 46
Caramel Apple Cider 47
Peppermint Hot Chocolate 48
BOOK 3: CHRISTMAS DRINK RECIPES 50
Crock Pot Creamy Hot Chocolate 51
Pumpkin Pie White Hot Chocolate 52
Easy Pumpkin Spice Latte 53
Peppermint Milkshake..54
White Peppermint Hot Chocolate 55
Chocolate Chip Peppermint Milkshake 56
Mocha Peppermint Frappe..57
Chocolate Peppermint Protein Shake 58
Peppermint Mocha...59
Caramel Apple Cider...60
Crock Pot Apple Cider...61
Peppermint Eggnog 62
Eggnog 63
Red Velvet Hot Chocolate..64
Caramel Hot Chocolate..65
Grinch Punch 66
Spiced White Chocolate Cocoa...67

Cookies and Cream Hot Chocolate	68
Crock Pot Mint Hot Chocolate	69
S'mores Hot Chocolate	70
BOOK 4: CHRISTMAS COCKTAILS	72
Hot Buttered Rum	73
Gingerbread Martini	74
Kahlua Hot Chocolate	75
Caramel Apple Sangria	76
S'mores Hot Chocolate	77
Andes Mint Hot Chocolate	78
Andes Peppermint Hot Chocolate	79
Spiced Eggnog	80
Cookies and Cream Hot Chocolate	81
Dirty Santa	82
Holiday White Wine Spritzer	83
Caramel Apple Hot Toddy	84
The Grinch	85
Holiday Sangria	86
Cranberry Mimosa	87
FREE GIFT	89
NOTES	90

FREE GIFT

Breakfast, Lunch, Dinner, Soups, Salads, Desserts and More!

To download your free eBook, simply visit:
www.Hanniepscott.com/freegift

Abbreviations

oz = ounce
fl oz = fluid ounce
tsp = teaspoon
tbsp = tablespoon
ml = milliliter
c = cup
pt = pint
qt = quart
gal = gallon
L = liter

Conversions

1/2 fl oz = 3 tsp = 1 tbsp = 15 ml
1 fl oz = 2 tbsp = 1/8 c = 30 ml
2 fl oz = 4 tbsp = 1/4 c = 60 ml
4 fl oz = 8 tbsp = 1/2 c = 118 ml
8 fl oz = 16 tbsp = 1 c = 236 ml
16 fl oz = 1 pt = 1/2 qt = 2 c = 473 ml
128 fl oz = 8 pt = 4 qt = 1 gal = 3.78 L

BOOK 1: CROCK POT RECIPES

Sausage Breakfast Casserole

Serves: 6-8

What you need:
1 lb of cooked ground sausage
12 eggs
1 cup milk
1 1/2 cups shredded cheddar cheese
1 tbsp ground mustard
1 32-oz bag shredded hash browns
Salt and pepper, to taste

What to do:
1. In a large bowl, beat the eggs and add in the milk, salt, pepper, and ground mustard.
2. In your slow cooker, make a layer of sausage, shredded hash browns, and cheese. Repeat the layers once.
3. Pour the egg mixture over the layers.
4. Cook on low for 8 hours (while you sleep!)
5. Top with cheese before serving.

French Toast

Servings: 4-6

What you need:
½ loaf of white bread
6 eggs
1 cup milk
1 tsp cinnamon
1 tbsp brown sugar
1 tsp vanilla

What to do:
1. Spray your crock pot with non-stick cooking spray.
2. In a large mixing bowl, whisk together the eggs, milk, cinnamon, brown sugar, and vanilla.
3. Dip each slice of bread into the egg mixture and then place it in your crock pot.
4. Pour any remaining egg mixture on top of the bread in the crock pot.
5. Cook on low 6-8 hours.
6. Serve with fresh fruit, whipped cream, or syrup.

Cinnamon Pecans

Servings: 4-6

What you need:
1 1/4 cup sugar
1 1/4 cup brown sugar
2 tbsp cinnamon
1/8 tsp salt
1 egg white
2 tsp vanilla
3 cups pecans
1/4 cup water

What to do:
1. In a large bowl, mix together the sugar, brown sugar, cinnamon, and salt.
2. In a separate bowl, mix together the egg white and vanilla.
3. Add the pecans to the egg mixture and coat them thoroughly.
4. Add the cinnamon mixture to the pecans and stir until they are evenly coated.
5. Pour the pecan mixture into your crockpot and cook on low for 3-4 hours, stirring occasionally.

Apple Crisp

Servings: 4

What you need:
5 large apples; peeled, cored, and sliced
1 tsp nutmeg
1 tsp cinnamon
1 tbsp maple syrup
1 tbsp lemon juice
1 cup oats
1/2 cup brown sugar
1/2 cup all-purpose flour
4 tbsp butter
1/4 tsp salt

What to do:
1. Add the sliced apples, half the nutmeg, half the cinnamon, maple syrup, and lemon juice to your crock pot and mix together well.
2. In a mixing bowl, mix together the oats, butter, sugar, flour, the other half the nutmeg, the other half of cinnamon. Spread this mixture over the apples in the crock pot.
3. Cook on low for 4 hours before serving.

Gingerbread Pudding

Servings: 8-10

What you need:
1 14-oz package of gingerbread mix
1/2 cup milk
1/2 cup raisins
2 1/4 cups water
1 cup packed brown sugar
3/4 cup butter

What to do:
1. Coat your crock pot with non-stick cooking spray.
2. In a medium bowl, combine the gingerbread mix and milk. Stir in the raisins. Spread the mixture into your crock pot.
3. In a saucepan over medium-high heat, combine the water, brown sugar, and butter. Bring to a boil, reduce heat, and simmer for 5 minutes.
4. Pour the sugar mixture over the batter in the crock pot.
5. Cook for 2 hours.
6. Turn off the crock pot and let it sit for 1 hour without the lid.
7. Serve with vanilla ice cream.

Carrot Cake

Servings: 8-10

What you need:

1 cup sugar
2 eggs
1/4 cup water
1/3 cup vegetable oil
1 1/2 cups flour
1 tsp vanilla
1 tsp baking powder
1/2 tsp baking soda
1 tsp cinnamon
1 cup packed grated carrots
Cream cheese frosting

What to do:

1. In a mixing bowl, cream the sugar, eggs, water and oil. Add the flour, vanilla, baking powder, baking soda, and cinnamon. Blend until combined. Stir in the carrots by hand.
2. Spray the inside of your crock pot with non-stick cooking spray.
3. Pour the batter into your crock pot and spread it evenly.
4. Cook for 2-3 hours on low or until a toothpick inserted into the middle comes out clean.
5. Remove the cake from the crock pot, let it cool, and top it with cream cheese frosting.

Christmas Crack

Servings: 10-12

What you need:
8 oz unsalted peanuts
8 oz salted peanuts
6 oz semi-sweet chocolate chips
6 oz milk chocolate chips
10 oz peanut butter chips
1 lb white almond bark

What to do:
1. Layer all ingredients in your crock pot, with the peanuts on the bottom.
2. Cover and cook on low for 2 hours.
3. Stir well and let cook for another 30 minutes to 1 hour.
4. Stir again then spoon the mixture onto wax paper or parchment paper.
5. Let cool for at least 1 hour.

Corn Casserole

Serves: 6-8

What you need:
8 oz cream cheese, softened
2 eggs, beaten
1/2 cup sugar
8 1/2 oz corn muffin mix
2 1/2 cups frozen corn
16 oz canned cream corn
1 cup milk
2 tbsp butter
1 tsp Cajun seasoning
Salt and pepper, to taste

What to do:
1. In a mixing bowl, combine the cream cheese, egg, and sugar.
2. Mix in the muffin mix, corn, milk, butter, and seasonings.
3. Pour the mixture into the crock pot and cook for 2-4 hours on high.
4. Season with salt and pepper if needed before serving.

Sweet Potatoes

Serves: 4

What you need:
4 medium sized sweet potatoes
Butter
Brown sugar
Mini marshmallows

What to do:
1. Scrub, wash, and dry the sweet potatoes.
2. Poke each potato with a fork several times.
3. Wrap each potato in foil twice.
4. Place potatoes in crock pot and cook on high for 4 hours or on low for 8 hours.
5. Top with butter, brown sugar, and mini marshmallows before serving.

Green Beans and New Potatoes

Serves: 6-8

What you need:
3 lbs fresh or frozen green beans
4-5 slices bacon, chopped
12 small new potatoes
2 cups chicken broth
1 small yellow onion, diced
1/4 cup butter
Salt and pepper, to taste

What to do:
1. Place all of the ingredients in your crock pot and gently combine.
2. Cook on low for 3-5 hours.

Squash and Apples
Serves: 6-8

What you need:
1 ~3-lb butternut squash; peeled, seeded, and cubed
4 apples, cored and chopped
3/4 cup dried cranberries
1 small yellow onion, diced
1 tbsp cinnamon
1 1/2 tsp ground nutmeg

What to do:
1. Combine the squash, apples, cranberries, onion, cinnamon, and nutmeg in your crock pot.
2. Cook on high for 4 hours or until the squash is tender.

Crustless Chicken Pot Pie

Serves: 4-6

What you need:

1 can cream of chicken soup

1 can cream of mushroom soup

2 14-oz bags of frozen mixed vegetables

1 tsp oregano

1 tsp dried basil

1 tsp garlic powder

2 cups heavy cream

1 1/2 lbs boneless skinless chicken breasts, chopped

Salt and pepper, to taste

3 cups rice

What to do:

1. Place all of the ingredients in a slow cooker and stir well.
2. Cook on high for 5-6 hours or on low for 8 hours.

Corn Chowder

Serves: 4-6

What you need:
16 oz canned whole kernel corn, drained
2 potatoes, peeled and chopped
1 onion, chopped
1/4 cup butter
2 cups milk
2 cups chicken broth
Salt and pepper, to taste
1 tbsp chopped parsley

What to do:
1. Combine all of the ingredients except 1/2 cup of corn, butter, and milk in your crock pot.
2. Cook on low for 7-9 hours, then puree in a blender, food processor, or with an immersion blender and return to the crock pot.
3. Stir in the extra half cup of corn, butter, and milk.
4. Cook on low for another hour before serving.

Turkey Breast

Servings: 18

What you need:
3 1/2 lb – 5 lb turkey breast
1/4 cup olive oil
1/2 tsp salt
1/2 tsp pepper
1 tsp garlic powder
1/2 tsp dried parsley
1 large onion, chopped
1 apple, cored and sliced
2 cups chicken broth

What to do:
1. Make sure there aren't any giblets inside the cavity of the turkey breast.
2. Wash and dry the chicken breast.
3. Brush the breast with olive oil and sprinkle on the salt, pepper, garlic powder, and parsley.
4. Place the chopped onion and apple into the turkey's cavity.
5. Place the turkey breast into your greased crock pot, breast side up.
6. Pour the chicken broth over the turkey.
7. Insert a meat thermometer into the thickest part of the turkey breast.
8. Cook for 3-4 hours or until the thermometer reaches 140 degrees F.
9. Cook for another 2-3 hours on low until the thermometer reaches 170 degrees F.

10. Remove the turkey from the crock pot and place it on a roasting pan.
11. Broil the turkey for 5-7 minutes or until the skin has browned.
12. Remove from the oven and let the turkey rest for 15 minutes.
13. Remove the onion and apple from the turkey.
14. Slice the turkey and serve.

Jambalaya

Serves: 6-8

What you need:
1 lb boneless skinless chicken breasts
1/2 lb Andouille sausage, diced
1 28-oz can diced tomatoes
1 can rotel tomatoes
1 yellow onion, chopped
1 green bell pepper, chopped
1 stalk celery, chopped
2 cups chicken broth
2 tsp dried oregano
2 tsp cajun seasoning
2 bay leaves
2 cups white long grain rice
Fresh parsley

What to do:
1. In the crock pot, combine all of the ingredients except the rice and parsley.
2. Cook on low for high for 4 hours.
3. Remove chicken, shred it, and return it to the crock pot.
4. Add rice to the crock pot and stir.
5. Cook on low for 2-4 hours or until rice is cooked. Stir occasionally.
6. Discard the bay leaves and top with parsley before serving.

Easy Christmas Ham

Servings: 10

What you need:
7-8 lb spiral cut ham
1 cup brown sugar
1/2 cup maple syrup
2 cups pineapple

What to do:
1. Place the ham inside your crock pot, flat side down.
2. Rub the brown sugar all over the ham.
3. Pour the maple syrup and pineapple over the ham.
4. Cover and cook on low for 4-6 hours, basting the liquid over the ham every hour or so.
5. Remove the ham from the crock pot and let it sit for 15 minutes before cutting and serving.

Cranberry Apple Butter

Servings: 18

What you need:
16-20 apples; peeled, cored, and sliced
12 oz fresh cranberries
3 3/4 cups sugar
1 tbsp cinnamon
1/4 tsp cloves
6-8 pint jars (depending on how big your crock pot is)

What to do:
1. Put the cranberries and apples in your crock pot and turn your crock pot on high.
2. Cook for 18 hours.
3. Add the sugar, cinnamon, and cloves. Stir well and cook for another 4 hours.
4. Spoon the apple butter into the jars, screw on the lids and rings, and let them cool on the counter.

Cornbread Dressing

Servings: 15

What you need:
6 cups cornbread
8 slices day old bread
4 eggs
1 onion, chopped
1/2 cup chopped celery
1 1/2 tbsp poultry seasoning
1/2 tsp black pepper
2 10-oz cans cream of chicken soup
1 10-oz cans chicken broth
1/3 cup butter
Salt and pepper, to taste

What to do:
1. Crumble the cornbread and the day old bread.
2. Spray your crock pot with non-stick spray.
3. Add all of the ingredients except the butter, salt, and pepper to your crock pot and stir together.
4. Dot the butter over the dressing and season with salt and pepper.
5. Cover and cook on high for 2 hours or on low for 4 hours.

BOOK 2: SLOW COOKER RECIPES

Pumpkin Spice Oatmeal

Servings: 4

What you need:
1 ½ cups milk
1 ½ cups water
1 cup steel cut oats
½ cup maple syrup
¾ cup pumpkin puree
1 ½ tbsp. pumpkin pie spice
½ cup applesauce
1 tsp vanilla
¼ tsp salt
1 cup toasted pecans

What to do:
1. Spray the inside of your slow cooker with non-stick spray.
2. Combine all of the ingredients except the toasted pecans in a large bowl and mix together well.
3. Pour the mixture into your slow cooker.
4. Cover and cook on low for 4-5 hours.
5. Stir the oatmeal and leave uncovered for 30 minutes to allow it to thicken.
6. Sprinkle the toasted pecans on top before serving.

Cinnamon Roll Casserole

Servings: 6-8

What you need:
2 12-oz cans of cinnamon rolls, icing reserved
4 eggs
½ cup whipping cream
3 tbsp maple syrup
2 tsp vanilla
1 tsp cinnamon
¼ tsp nutmeg

What to do:
1. Spray your slow cooker with non-stick spray.
2. Unroll the cinnamon rolls from the cans and cut each roll into 4 pieces.
3. Place a layer of the cinnamon roll pieces in the bottom of your slow cooker.
4. In a medium bowl, whisk together the eggs, cream, maple syrup, vanilla, cinnamon, and nutmeg.
5. Pour this mixture evenly over the layer of cinnamon roll pieces in the bottom of your slow cooker.
6. Place the remaining cinnamon roll pieces in the slow cooker and spoon one container of the icing over the rolls.
7. Cover and cook on low for 2-3 hours or until the rolls are set.
8. Drizzle the remaining container of icing over the rolls.
9. Serve warm.

Candied Pecans

Servings: 16

What you need:
1 cup sugar
3/4 cup brown sugar
1 1/2 tbsp cinnamon
1 egg white
2 tsp vanilla
4 cups pecans
1/4 cup water

What to do:
1. In a large bowl, mix together the sugar, brown sugar, and cinnamon.
2. In a separate bowl, whisk together the egg white and vanilla until it is a little bit frothy.
3. Spray your slow cooker with cooking spray.
4. Put the pecans in the slow cooker.
5. Pour the egg mixture over the pecans and stir well.
6. Sprinkle the cinnamon sugar mixture over the pecans and stir well.
7. Cover and cook on low for 3 hours, stirring every 30 minutes.
8. When there are 30 minutes left, pour 1/4 cup water into the slow cooker and stuff.
9. Spread the pecans on a baking pan and let them cool for 15-20 minutes.

Monkey Bread

Servings: 10

What you need:
1 16-oz roll biscuits
1/2 cup sugar
1/2 cup brown sugar
1 tsp cinnamon
1 stick butter, melted
4 oz cream cheese, cubed and softened

What to do:
1. Spray the inside of your slow cooker with non-stick spray.
2. Combine the sugar, brown sugar, and cinnamon in a gallon zip lock bag and set aside.
3. Cut each biscuit into 6 pieces.
4. Dip each biscuit piece into the melted butter.
5. Place dipped biscuits into the gallon zip lock bag with the sugar mixture and shake well to coat.
6. Pour any remaining butter into your slow cooker.
7. Transfer all biscuit pieces to your slow cooker.
8. Cook on low for 2-3 hours or until dough is done.
9. Stir in cubed cream cheese before serving.

Bread Pudding

Serves: 4-6

What you need:
10 slices raisin cinnamon swirl bread, cut into cubes
1 14-oz can sweetened condensed milk
1 cup water
1 tsp vanilla
5 eggs, beaten

What to do:
1. Place the bread cubes into your slow cooker.
2. Mix the sweetened condensed milk, water, vanilla, and eggs together in a bowl and pour the mixture over the bread.
3. Stir to coat the bread evenly.
4. Cook on low for 3-4 hours or until set.

Fudge

Servings: 8-10

What you need:
1 cup dark chocolate chips
1 cup of coconut milk
1/4 cup of honey

What to do:
1. Mix the ingredients directly into your slow cooker.
2. Cook on low for 2 hours.
3. Stir until the mixture is smooth.
4. Pour the fudge mixture into a greased casserole dish.
5. Cover the fudge with plastic wrap and refrigerate for at least 3 hours before serving.

Pumpkin Pie

Servings: 6

What you need:
1 15-oz can of pumpkin
2/3 cup cinnamon bun flavored coffee creamer
2 tbsp pumpkin pie spice (divided)
1 9-oz yellow cake mix
1 cup chopped pecans
1/4 cup butter

What to do:
1. Spray the inside of your slow cooker with non-stick spray.
2. In a medium bowl, mix together the pumpkin, coffee creamer, and 1 tbsp of pumpkin pie spice.
3. Spread the mixture into your slow cooker.
4. In a separate bowl, mix together the cake mix, pecans, and 1 tsp pumpkin pie spice.
5. Sprinkle the mixture over the pumpkin mixture in your slow cooker.
6. Drizzle the melted butter over the top of the dry mixture.
7. Cover and cook on high for 2 1/2 hours.
8. Serve warm.

Sweet Potato Mash

Serves: 6-8

What you need:
2 lbs sweet potatoes, peeled and chopped
1/2 cup apple juice
1 tbsp ground cinnamon
1 tbsp sugar
1 tbsp brown sugar
1 tsp ground nutmeg
1/2 cup apple juice
1 cup pecans

What to do:
1. Place all of the ingredients except the pecans and the second half cup of apple juice in your slow cooker.
2. Cook on low for 4-5 hours or until the potatoes are tender.
3. When potatoes are tender, mash everything in the slow cooker with a potato masher.
4. Pour in the second half cup of apple juice and mash more.
5. Top with pecans before serving.

Cheddar Creamed Corn

Serves: 6-8

What you need:
32-oz of frozen corn
1 8-oz block of cream cheese, cubed
1 cup shredded cheddar cheese
1/4 cup butter
1/2 cup heavy cream
1/2 tsp salt
1/2 tsp pepper

What to do:
1. Place all of the ingredients in your slow cooker and stir well.
2. Cook on low for 3-4 hours or until cream cheese is melted.
3. Stir well and serve.

Sweet Potato Casserole

Serves: 8-10

What you need:
2 29-oz cans sweet potatoes, drained
1/2 cup brown sugar
1 tbsp cinnamon
1 stick butter, sliced
1/2 cup heavy cream
1 cup crushed pecans
3 tbsp brown sugar

What to do:
1. Place drained sweet potatoes into slow cooker.
2. Pour in the heavy cream.
3. Sprinkle brown sugar and cinnamon on top.
4. Place butter slices on top.
5. Cook on low for 4 hours.
6. After 4 hours, mash up the sweet potatoes really well and stir everything together.
7. Sprinkle with crushed pecans and brown sugar.
8. Cover and let it cook for another 20-30 minutes before serving.

Butternut Squash

Serves: 2-3

What you need:
1 large butternut squash

What to do:
1. Wrap the squash in aluminum foil and cook in your slow cooker on high for 4 hours or low for 6 hours.
2. Remove the squash from the aluminum foil and let it cool for 15-20 minutes.
3. Unwrap the squash and slice it in half lengthwise.
4. Scoop the seeds out with a spoon.
5. Scoop the soft squash flesh out of the skin and serve it or place it in an airtight container and refrigerate.

Hash Brown Casserole

Servings: 10-12

What you need:
32 oz bag of frozen hash browns
8 oz sour cream
10.5 oz cream of mushroom soup
¼ cup finely chopped onion
2 cups shredded cheddar cheese
½ cup butter, melted
Salt and pepper, to taste

What to do:
1. Slightly break apart the frozen hash browns.
2. Spray your slow cooker with non-stick spray.
3. In your slow cooker, mix together the hash browns, sour cream, cream of mushroom soup, onion, cheese, and melted butter.
4. Sprinkle the mixture with salt and pepper and cook for 4-5 hours on low.

Vegetable Stew

Serves: 6-8

What you need:
2 yellow onions, diced
3 stalks celery, diced
2 large carrots, sliced
3 potatoes, peeled and diced
1 cup mushrooms, cleaned and chopped
1/4 cup lentils
3 cloves garlic, minced
1/2 tsp grated ginger
1/2 tsp thyme
1 bay leaf
2 cups water
1/4 cup soy sauce
Salt and pepper, to taste
Cornstarch

What to do:
1. Place the onions, celery, carrots, potatoes, mushrooms, lentils, garlic, ginger, thyme, bay leaf, water, and soy sauce in your slow cooker.
2. Cook for 10-12 hours on low.
3. Around 8-10 hours, add the salt, pepper, and a little bit of corn starch if you want your stew to be thicker.

Baked Potato Soup

Serves: 8-10

What you need:
5 lbs russet potatoes, washed and diced
1 yellow onion, diced
5 cloves garlic, minced
2 quarts chicken broth
2 8-oz blocks cream cheese
1 tsp salt
1 tsp bacon
Crumbled bacon
Shredded cheese
Chopped green onion

What to do:
1. Add the potatoes, onion, garlic, chicken broth, and salt to a slow cooker.
2. Cook on high for 6-7 hours.
3. Cube and soften the cream cheese and add it to the slow cooker.
4. Use a potato masher to mash up the potatoes and cream cheese.
5. Stir well and cook on low for another 2 hours.
6. Top with bacon, cheese, and green onion before serving.

Chicken and Dumplings

Serves: 6-8

What you need:
4 skinless chicken thighs
4 skinless chicken drumsticks
1 quart chicken broth
3 cups water
1 small yellow onion, diced
1 stalk celery, chopped
1 tsp dried thyme
1/4 tsp salt
1 12-oz package frozen dumplings
2 tsp butter
1 tsp freshly ground black pepper

What to do:
1. Boil the chicken thighs and drumsticks in chicken broth and water for 45 minutes.
2. Remove the chicken from the liquid and let it cool slightly.
3. Shred the chicken off of the bones.
4. Pour the liquid into the slow cooker and set to high.
5. Separate the dumpling strips and break each strip in half.
6. Add the dumplings to the slow cooker one at a time.
7. Add the chicken, onion, celery, thyme, salt, butter, and pepper to the slow cooker.
8. Let the chicken and dumplings cook on high for 2 hours, stirring occasionally.
9. Reduce heat to low and let cook for another 2-4 hours on low.

Christmas Ham

Serves: 4-6

What you need:
1 precooked, spiral cut ham
2 cups brown sugar
1 can pineapple rings

What to do:
1. Sprinkle 1 and 1/2 cups of the brown sugar into the bottom of a slow cooker.
2. Place the ham on top of the brown sugar and pour the pineapple rings and juice on top.
3. Sprinkle the rest of the brown sugar on top of the ham.
4. Cook for 6-8 hours on low.

Cranberry Sauce

Servings: 20

What you need:
1 12-oz bag of cranberries
1/4 cup water
3/4 cup orange marmalade
3/4 cup sugar
1/4 sp cinnamon

What to do:
1. Place all of the ingredients in your slow cooker and stir together.
2. Cook on high for 3 hours or until the cranberries begin to burst.
3. Once they begin to burst, gently mash the mixture with a potato masher.

Stuffing

Servings: 14

What you need:
12 cups dry bread cubes
4 stalks celery, chopped
1/2 cup chopped fresh parsley
2 tsp dried sage
1/2 tsp dried thyme
1/2 tsp salt
1/4 tsp black pepper
1 3/4 cup chicken broth
1/3 cup butter, melted

What to do:
1. Combine all the ingredients in your slow cooker, adding the chicken broth and melted butter last. Mix well.
2. Cook on low for 4-6 hours.

Nutella Hot Chocolate

Servings: 4-6

What you need:

5 cups milk
1/2 cup cocoa powder
1/2 cup Nutella
1/2 cup sugar
1 cup water

What to do:

1. Combine the cocoa, Nutella, sugar, and water in a large pan on your stove. Stir and bring to a gentle boil until the sugar and cocoa are dissolved.
2. Pour the mixture into your crock pot.
3. Add the milk to your crock pot and stir.
4. Cook on high for 2 hours or on low for 4 hours.
5. Pour into mugs and serve.

Caramel Apple Cider

Servings: 12

What you need:
12 cups apple juice
6 cinnamon sticks
1/2 cup caramel sauce
Whipped cream

What to do:
1. Place the cinnamon sticks and apple juice in your crock pot and cook for 4 hours on high.
2. Stir in the caramel sauce and serve in mugs topped with whipped cream.

Peppermint Hot Chocolate

Servings: 4-6

What you need:
5 cups milk
1/2 cup cocoa powder
1/2 cup sugar
1 cup water
4 tsp peppermint syrup

What to do:
1. Combine the cocoa, sugar, and water in a large pan on your stove. Stir and bring to a gentle boil until the sugar and cocoa are dissolved.
2. Pour the mixture into your crock pot.
3. Add the milk and peppermint syrup to your crock pot and stir.
4. Cook on high for 2 hours or on low for 4 hours.
5. Pour into mugs and serve.

BOOK 3: CHRISTMAS DRINK RECIPES

Crock Pot Creamy Hot Chocolate

Servings: 8-10

What you need:
14-oz can of sweetened condensed milk
1 1/2 cups heavy whipping cream
6 cups milk
1 1/2 tsp vanilla
2 cups chocolate chips

What to do:
1. Pour all of the ingredients into your crock pot and stir together well.
2. Cover and cook on low for 2 hours, stirring occasionally.
3. Serve topped with marshmallows.

Pumpkin Pie White Hot Chocolate

Servings: 2

What you need:
2 cups milk
1/2 cup white chocolate chips
2 tbsp canned pumpkin
1 tbsp corn starch
1 tbsp vanilla extract
Marshmallows

What to do:
1. In a medium saucepan over low heat, add the milk, chocolate chips, pumpkin, corn starch, and vanilla extract.
2. Whisk together until combined and let simmer for 5-7 minutes or until chocolate is melted and liquid is thickened.
3. Pour into two coffee mugs.
4. Top with marshmallows before serving.

Easy Pumpkin Spice Latte

Servings: 2

What you need:
1/2 cup pumpkin puree
1 cup French vanilla liquid coffee creamer
2 tsp pumpkin pie spice
1 1/2 cups hot strong coffee
Whipped cream
Cinnamon

What to do:
1. In a medium saucepan over medium heat, whisk together the pumpkin puree, coffee creamer, and pumpkin pie spice until smooth.
2. Reduce the heat to low and simmer for 5 minutes.
3. Pour in the coffee.
4. Pour into coffee mugs and top with whipped cream and cinnamon.
5. Serve immediately.

Peppermint Milkshake

Servings: 1-2

What you need:
3 large scoops of vanilla bean ice cream
1/2 tsp peppermint extract
3/4 cup milk
Whipped cream
1 candy cane, crushed

What to do:
1. In a blender, blend the ice cream, milk, and peppermint extract.
2. Top with whipped cream and crushed candy canes.

White Peppermint Hot Chocolate

Servings: 4

What you need:
2/3 cup heavy whipping cream
8 peppermints, crushed
4 cups milk
8 oz white chocolate, chopped
1/2 tsp peppermint extract
Crushed peppermints, for garnish

What to do:
1. In a medium bowl with a mixer, beat the heavy whipping cream and crushed peppermints until stiff peaks form. Cover and refrigerate.
2. In a large saucepan, heat the milk over medium heat.
3. Add the white chocolate to the milk and whisk until it is melted completely.
4. Stir in the peppermint extract.
5. Ladle the hot chocolate into mugs and top with the whipped cream mixture from the refrigerator.
6. Top the whipped cream with crushed peppermints and serve.

Chocolate Chip Peppermint Milkshake

Servings: 2

What you need:
2 cups vanilla ice cream
1/2 cup milk
1 tsp peppermint extract
4 candy canes, crushed
1/4 cup chocolate chips
Whipped cream
Extra crushed candy canes

What to do:
1. Put the ice cream, milk, peppermint extract, and crushed candy canes in your blender and blend until smooth.
2. Add in the chocolate chips and pulse for a few seconds.
3. Pour into a cup or cups and top with whipped cream and the extra crushed candy canes.

Mocha Peppermint Frappe

Servings: 1-2

What you need:
1 1/2 cups strong brewed coffee, partially frozen
1/2 cup milk
2 tsp unsweetened cocoa powder
1 tsp stevia (or to taste)
1/2 tsp peppermint extract
Whipped cream
Crushed peppermints

What to do:
1. In your blender, combine the coffee, milk, cocoa powder, stevia, and peppermint extract until smooth.
2. Pour into a glass and top with whipped cream and crushed peppermints.

Chocolate Peppermint Protein Shake

Servings: 1

What you need:
1 large banana, frozen
2-3 large ice cubes
1 cup milk
1 scoop chocolate protein powder
2 tbsp cocoa powder
Pinch of sea salt
1/4 tsp peppermint extract
1 tbsp dark chocolate chips
Whipped cream

What to do:
1. Place all of the ingredients except the whipped cream in your blender and blend until smooth.
2. Pour into a glass and top with whipped cream.

Peppermint Mocha

Servings: 1

What you need:
1/4 cup sugar
1/4 cup water
1/4 tsp peppermint extract
3 tbsp powdered cocoa
3 tbsp hot water
1/2 cup hot espresso or strong brewed coffee
1 1/2 cup steamed milk
Whipped cream

What to do:
1. In a small saucepan over medium heat, stir together the water and sugar. Bring to a boil and let the sugar dissolve. Reduce heat to a simmer and add the peppermint extract. Let simmer for 20 minutes.
2. Mix the cocoa and 3 tbsp of hot water in a mug until a paste forms.
3. Add the espresso and the sugar/water/peppermint mixture to the mug and stir well.
4. Add the milk, stir, and serve.
5. Top with whipped cream.

Caramel Apple Cider

Serves: 2

What you need:
3 tbsp cinnamon dulce syrup
12 oz apple juice or store bought apple cider
Whipped cream
Caramel sauce

What to do:
1. Pour the 3 tbsp of cinnamon dulce syrup in a small saucepan over medium heat.
2. Add 12 oz of apple juice or apple cider to the saucepan and bring to a simmer.
3. Add the cider to a mug and top with whipped cream and caramel sauce.
4. Serve immediately.

Crock Pot Apple Cider

Servings: 20+

What you need:
2 quarts store bought apple cider
1/4 cup brown sugar
1/8 tsp ground ginger
1 orange, unpeeled and cut into wedges
2 cinnamon sticks
1 tsp whole cloves
Cheesecloth

What to do:
1. Tie up the cinnamon sticks and whole clothes in the cheesecloth.
2. Add all of the ingredients to your crock pot.
3. Cover and cook on low for 3 hours.
4. Remove the cheesecloth bag and the orange wedges before serving.
5. Store any leftovers in the refrigerator and reheat before serving.

Peppermint Eggnog

Serves: 6-8

What you need:
1 quart eggnog
3/4 cup white chocolate chips
1/3 cup crushed candy canes
Whipped cream
Extra crushed candy canes

What to do:
1. In a saucepan over medium heat, combine the eggnog, white chocolate chips, and crushed candy canes in a saucepan. Stir occasionally and heat until the white chocolate is melted.
2. Pour into mugs and top with whipped cream and crushed candy canes.

Eggnog

Serves: 3-4

What you need:
6 large egg yolks
1/2 cup sugar
1 cup heavy cream
2 cups milk
1 1/2 tsp freshly grated nutmeg
A pinch of salt
1/4 tsp vanilla extract
1/8 tsp rum extract

What to do:
1. In a large bowl, whisk together the egg yolks and sugar until creamy.
2. In a large saucepan over medium heat, stir together the heavy cream, milk, nutmeg and salt and bring to a simmer. Stir often.
3. Ladle 1/2 cup of the cream/milk mixture into the egg mixture and whisk vigorously.
4. Ladle in another 1/2 cup of the cream/milk mixture and whisk vigorously. Repeat until all of the cream/milk mixture has been added to the egg mixture.
5. Pour the mixture back into the saucepan over medium heat and continuously whisk until it reaches 160 degrees F on a thermometer.
6. Remove from the heat and stir in the vanilla extract and rum extract.
7. Pour into a pitcher or bowl and refrigerate until chilled.

Red Velvet Hot Chocolate

Serves: 4

What you need:
4 cups whole milk
1/4 cup sugar
10 oz chocolate chips
2 tsp red food coloring
1 tsp vanilla extract
Whipped cream

What to do:
1. In a medium saucepan over medium heat, add the milk and sugar and stir until the sugar is dissolved and the mixture is heated thoroughly.
2. Remove from the heat and stir in the chocolate until it is melted. Stir in the food coloring and vanilla extract.
3. Pour the mixture into mugs and top with whipped cream.

Caramel Hot Chocolate

Servings: 2

What you need:
2 cups whole milk
1/2 cup chocolate chips
1/2 cup caramel sauce
Marshmallows
Grated chocolate, as garnish
Caramel sauce, for drizzling

What to do:
1. In a medium sauce pan over medium heat, add the milk, chocolate chips, and caramel. Whisk until the chocolate chips are melted.
2. Serve warm topped with marshmallows, grated chocolate, and caramel sauce.

Grinch Punch

Servings: 16

What you need:
1/3 cup sugar
1/3 cup water
1/3 cup evaporated milk
1/2 tsp almond extract
12 drops neon green food coloring
2 liters lemon lime soda
1 pint vanilla ice cream
1 pint lime sherbet

What to do:
1. In a large saucepan over medium heat, combine the sugar and water and heat until the sugar is dissolved.
2. Remove the saucepan from the heat and stir in the evaporated milk and almond extract. Cover and refrigerate until chilled.
3. Pour the milk mixture into a large punch bowl. Stir in the food coloring and the lemon-lime soda.
4. Top with the vanilla ice cream and lime sherbet and serve.

Spiced White Chocolate Cocoa

Servings: 12

What you need:
16 oz good quality white chocolate, chopped
4 cups milk
4 cups heavy cream
1 tbsp vanilla extract
1/4 tsp ground nutmeg
3 cinnamon sticks
Whipped cream

What to do:
1. Place the white chocolate in the bottom of your crock pot.
2. Add all the remaining ingredients except the whipped cream to the crock pot and stir.
3. Cook on low for 2 hours, stirring occasionally.
4. Ladle into mugs and top with whipped cream to serve.

Cookies and Cream Hot Chocolate

Serves: 2

What you need:
2 cups milk
1/2 cup hot chocolate powder
5 Oreos, finely crushed
Whipped cream
Extra crushed Oreos for topping

What to do:
1. Heat the milk in a medium saucepan over medium heat but don't let it boil.
2. When the milk is simmering, add the hot chocolate powder.
3. Add the crushed Oreos to the milk.
4. Serve in a mug topped with whipped cream and crushed Oreos.

Crock Pot Mint Hot Chocolate

Serves: 16

What you need:
1 gallon of milk
20 mini peppermint patties, chopped
1 1/2 cups hot chocolate powder
1 tbsp vanilla
Whipped cream
Chocolate syrup

What to do:
1. Add all of the ingredients to your crock pot, except the whipped cream and chocolate syrup.
2. Heat on low for 2 hours, stirring occasionally.
3. Vigorously beat with a whisk to make the hot chocolate light and frothy.
4. Pour into mugs and top with whipped cream and chocolate syrup.

S'mores Hot Chocolate

Serves: 2-3

What you need:
3 cups milk
1/4 cup cocoa powder
2 tbsp chocolate syrup
2-3 tbsp sugar
A pinch of salt
Crushed graham crackers
1/2 cup marshmallows

What to do:
1. Preheat your oven to low broil and place a rack in the second to the highest position. Place a baking sheet on the rack.
2. In a saucepan over medium heat, heat the milk until warm but do not boil.
3. When milk is simmering, add the cocoa powder, chocolate syrup, sugar, and salt. Whisk vigorously.
4. Pour the hot chocolate into glass mugs.
5. Top the hot chocolate with 1/4 cup of marshmallows each.
6. Carefully place the mugs on the baking sheet in the oven and broil until the marshmallows are browned but not burned! Watch them carefully.
7. Carefully remove the mugs from the oven and sprinkle crushed graham crackers over the marshmallows.

BOOK 4: CHRISTMAS COCKTAILS

Hot Buttered Rum

Servings: 4

What you need:
2 cups water
1/2 stick butter
1/4 cup packed brown sugar
1 tsp cinnamon
1/2 tsp freshly grated nutmeg
1/4 tsp ground cloves
1/8 tsp salt
2/3 cup dark rum

What to do:
1. In a medium saucepan over medium-high heat, bring the water, butter, brown sugar, cinnamon, nutmeg, cloves, and salt to a boil.
2. Reduce heat and simmer, stirring occasionally, for 10 minutes.
3. Remove from the heat, stir in the rum, and serve.

Gingerbread Martini

Servings: 1

What you need:
1 1/2 oz vodka
1/2 oz brandy
2 oz coffee-mate gingerbread latte
Cinnamon, as garnish

What to do:
1. Shake all of the ingredients together in a shaker and strain into a chilled martini glass.
2. Garnish with cinnamon and serve.

Kahlua Hot Chocolate

Servings: 2

What you need:
2 cups whole milk
1/2 cup chocolate sauce
4 oz Kahlua
Whipped cream
Extra chocolate sauce for drizzling

What to do:
1. In a medium saucepan over medium heat, combine the milk and chocolate sauce. Bring to a simmer.
2. Remove from heat and stir in the Kahlua.
3. Transfer to mugs and top with whipped cream and drizzle with chocolate sauce.

Caramel Apple Sangria

Servings: 10-12

What you need:
1 750ml bottle of pinot grigio
1 cup caramel vodka
6 cups apple cider
2 medium apples, cored and sliced

What to do:
1. Stir the wine, vodka, and apple cider together in a large pitcher or punch bowl.
2. Add the chopped apples to the pitcher or punch bowl.
3. Serve over ice.

S'mores Hot Chocolate

Serves: 2-3

What you need:
3 cups milk
1/4 cup cocoa powder
2 tbsp chocolate syrup
2-3 tbsp sugar
A pinch of salt
½ cup Bailey's Irish Cream
Crushed graham crackers
1/2 cup marshmallows

What to do:
1. Preheat your oven to low broil and place a rack in the second to the highest position. Place a baking sheet on the rack.
2. In a saucepan over medium heat, heat the milk until warm but do not boil.
3. When milk is simmering, add the cocoa powder, chocolate syrup, sugar, and salt. Whisk vigorously.
4. Remove from heat and stir in the Bailey's.
5. Pour the hot chocolate into glass mugs.
6. Top the hot chocolate with 1/4 cup of marshmallows each.
7. Carefully place the mugs on the baking sheet in the oven and broil until the marshmallows are browned but not burned! Watch them carefully.
8. Carefully remove the mugs from the oven and sprinkle crushed graham crackers over the marshmallows.

Andes Mint Hot Chocolate

Servings: 4-5

What you need:
1 bag Andes crème de menthe baking chips
2 cups Rumchata
2 cups half and half
2 cups milk
Marshmallows

What to do:
1. Put all of the ingredients in your crock pot and cook on high for an hour, stirring occasionally.
2. Turn your crock pot to low or warm and serve topped with marshmallows.

Andes Peppermint Hot Chocolate

Servings: 4-5

What you need:
1 bag Andes mint peppermint crunch baking chips
2 cups Rumchata
2 cups half and half
2 cups milk
Marshmallows

What to do:
1. Put all of the ingredients in your crock pot and cook on high for an hour, stirring occasionally.
2. Turn your crock pot to low or warm and serve topped with marshmallows.

Spiced Eggnog

Makes about 1 quart

What you need:
1 quart store-bought eggnog
¼ cup spiced rum
¼ cup Kahlua
2 tbsp bourbon
½ tsp vanilla extract
Ground cinnamon
Ground cloves
Ground nutmeg
Brown sugar

What to do:
1. Place the eggnog, rum, Kahlua, bourbon, and vanilla in your blender and pulse for a few seconds.
2. Rim glasses with brown sugar.
3. Pour eggnog into each glass.
4. Sprinkle eggnog with cinnamon, cloves, and nutmeg.
5. Serve!

Cookies and Cream Hot Chocolate

Serves: 2

What you need:
2 cups milk
1/2 cup hot chocolate powder
1/2 cup Bailey's Irish Cream
5 Oreos, finely crushed
Whipped cream
Extra crushed Oreos for topping

What to do:
1. Heat the milk in a medium saucepan over medium heat but don't let it boil.
2. When the milk is simmering, add the hot chocolate powder.
3. Add the crushed Oreos to the milk.
4. Remove from the heat and stir in the Bailey's.
5. Serve in a mug topped with whipped cream and crushed Oreos.

Dirty Santa

Servings: 1

What you need:
4 oz coffee, frozen into ice cubes
4 oz Bailey's Irish Cream
1 oz vanilla vodka

What to do:
1. Place the coffee ice cubes in a glass.
2. Pour the Bailey's and vodka in a shaker and strain over the ice.
3. Serve!

Holiday White Wine Spritzer

Servings: 20+

What you need:
1.5 L of Barefoot Moscato White Wine
1 L of diet sprite
1 L of red cream soda
12 oz of frozen raspberries

What to do:
1. Pour the wine, sprite, and cream soda in a large pitcher or punch bowl.
2. Add the frozen raspberries and serve.

Caramel Apple Hot Toddy

Servings: 8-10

What you need:
1 ½ cups caramel vodka
½ gallon apple cider
½ cup bourbon
3 cinnamon sticks
Whipped cream

What to do:
1. In a saucepan over medium-low heat, mix together the vodka, cider, bourbon, and cinnamon sticks until heated through.
2. Ladle into mugs and top with whipped cream before serving.

The Grinch

Servings: 1

What you need:
1 large scoop of lime sherbet
1 cup of ginger ale
2 oz whipped cream vodka or regular vodka
Green decorating sugar

What to do:
1. Rim a tall glass with green decorating sugar.
2. In your blender, mix together the sherbet, ginger ale, and vodka.
3. Pour into the glass and serve.

Holiday Sangria

Servings: 20+

What you need:
1 bottle white wine
1 bottle sparkling cider
2 oranges, sliced
1 red apple, cored and chopped
1 green apple, cored and chopped
2 cups cranberries

What to do:
1. Combine the wine and cider in a pitcher.
2. Add all of the fruit.
3. Stir well and chill until ready to serve.

Cranberry Mimosa

Servings: 20+

What you need:
1 bottle cranberry juice
1 bottle sparkling white wine

What to do:
1. Mix the cranberry juice and sparkling wine together and pour into champagne glasses.
2. Serve!

FREE GIFT

Breakfast, Lunch, Dinner, Soups, Salads, Desserts and More!

To download your free eBook, simply visit:
www.Hanniepscott.com/freegift

NOTES

NOTES

NOTES

NOTES

Printed in Great Britain
by Amazon